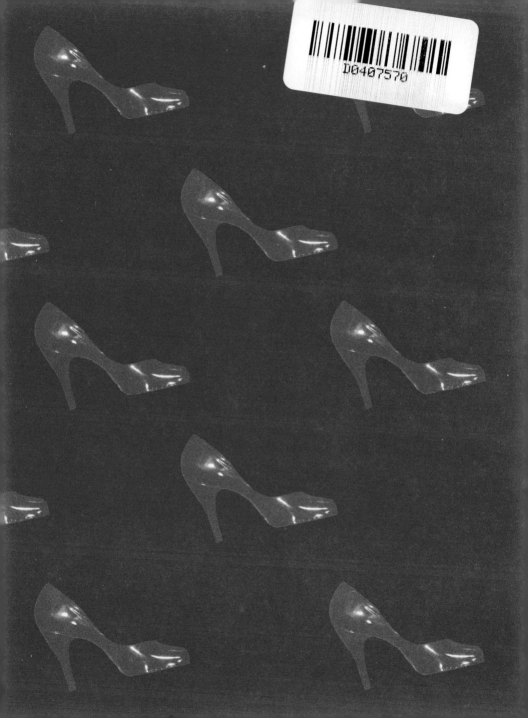

Shoes

Shoes

STEWART, TABORI & CHANG

NEW YORK

FUNCTION
VS.
STYLE

To be carried by shoes, winged by them. To wear dreams on one's feet is to begin to give reality to one's dreams.

ROGER VIVIER

Mama always said there's an awful lot you can tell about a person by their shoes: where they're going, where they've been.

ORREST GUMP

Not diamonds but heels are a girl's best friend.

WILLIAM ROSSI

I don't know who invented the high heel, but all women owe him a lot.

Marilyn Monroe

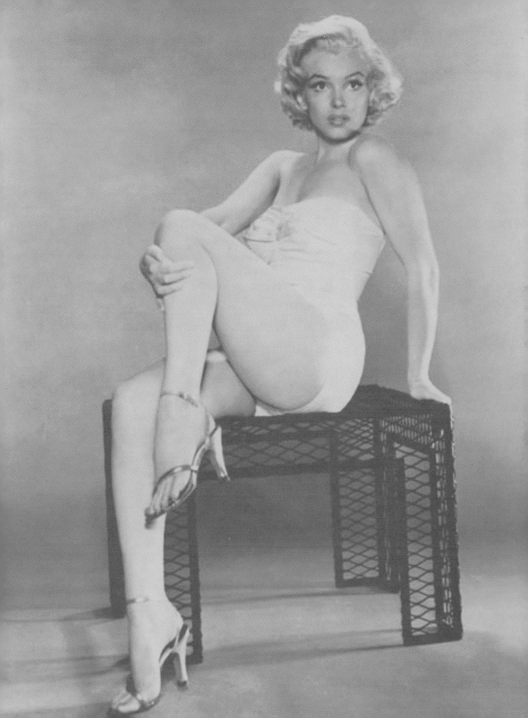

When in doubt, overdress.

Vivienne Westwood

15

Any WOMAN who, through the use of HIGHHEELED shoes or other devices, leads a subject of her Majesty into marriage shall be punished with the penalties of WITCHERY.

SEVENTEENTH CENTURY DECREE OF PARLIAMENT

17

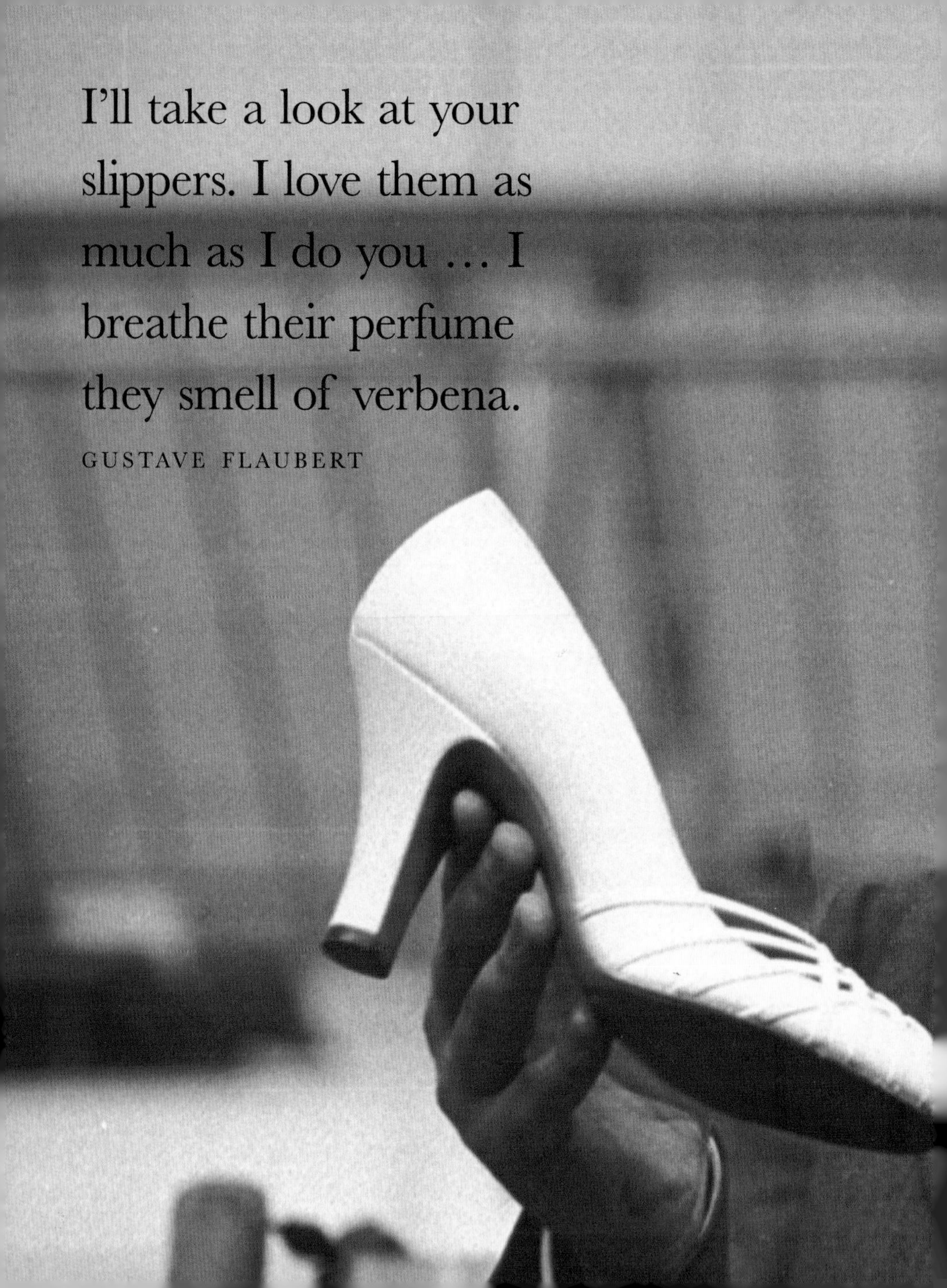

I'll take a look at your
slippers. I love them as
much as I do you ... I
breathe their perfume
they smell of verbena.

GUSTAVE FLAUBERT

east meets west

It is the flagrant lack of practicality that makes high-heeled shoes so fascinating.

STEPHEN BAYLEY

The girl with low and sensible heels is likely to pay for her bed and meals.

Saturday Evening Post

Shoe shine

WORK / STRI

GTH / FORM

A man cannot make a
pair of shoes rightly
unless he do it in
a devout manner.

Thomas Carlyle

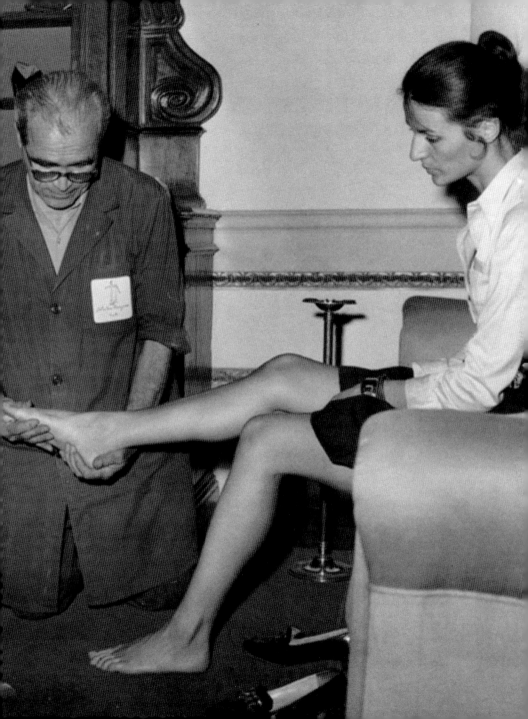

Nothing has been invented yet
that will do a better job than heels at
making a good pair of legs look great,
or great ones look fabulous.

STUART WEITZMAN

BIG FOOT

According to *Harper's Index*, the average increase in the protusion of a woman's buttocks when she wears high heels is 25%.

Shoes, like buildings, have a mysterious chemistry of proportion.

SUZANNE SLESIN

A **soldier** in **shoes** is only a soldier, but in **boots** he becomes a **warrior**.

GENERAL PATTON

BOOTLEG

ICON

Close your eyes and tap your heels together three times and think to yourself, "there's no place like home."

Dorothy in *The Wizard of Oz*

In matters of grave importance, STYLE, not sincerity, is the vital thing.

Oscar Wilde

*I have always steadfastly insisted on
pure silk for my shoes with double satin
ribbons, to tie round the ankle.
...I cannot accustom myself to dance
in any others.*

MARGOT FONTEYN

But don't you step on my
blue suede shoes
You can do anything but lay
off my blue suede shoes.

Carl Perkins

I didn't have
3,000 pairs of
shoes. I had
only 1,060

IMELDA MARCOS

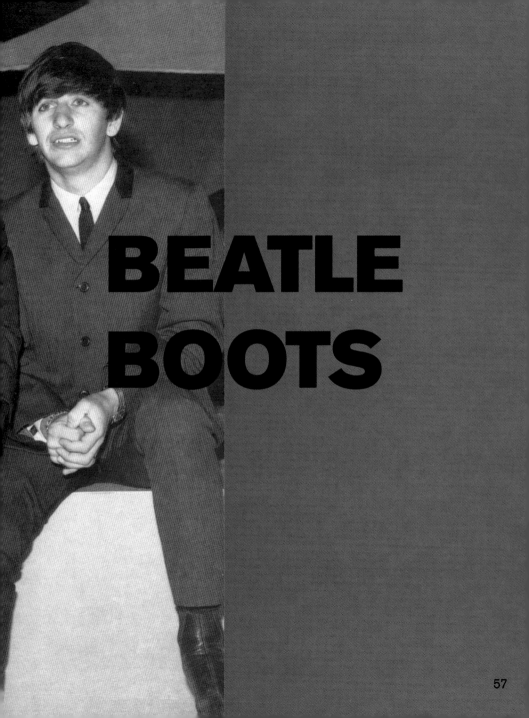

BEATLE BOOTS

ACTIVE

KICK

IT

Will you, won't you
Will you, won't you
Will you join the danc

**Lewis Carroll from *Alice's
Adventures in Wonderland***

. . . the Red Shoes are never tired. They dance . . . out into the street, they dance . . . over the mountains and valleys, through fields and forests, through night and day. Time rushes by, love rushes by, life rushes by but the Red Shoes go on.

BORIS LERMONTOV IN *THE RED SHOES*

jump

Please send me your last
pair of shoes, worn out with
dancing, as you mention in
your letter, so that I might
have something to press
against my heart.

GOETHE, in a letter to Christine Vulpius

Give a girl the
right shoes
and she can
conquer the
world.

BETTE MIDLER

Her feet, by half-a-mile of sea, In spotless sand left shapely prints...

Coventry Patmore

FOOTLOOSE

One should always have one's boots on and be ready to leave.

Michel de Montaigne

PICTURE CREDITS

page 4/5: Footwear from a London fashion show, 1963.

page 6: Roller skater, Long Island, New York, 1950.

page 8/9: Tramp's footwear, 1939.

page 10/11: Stiletto heels, 1953.

page 13: Marilyn Monroe, 1958.

page 14/15: Wellington boots, from, left to right, 1896, 1914, 1916 land girl, 1925 and 1928.

page 16/17: Seamed stockings, circa 1951.

page 18/19: British shoe manufacturer Edward Rayne, 1953.

page 20: Platform shoes with eight-inch heels, London, 1972.

page 21: Geisha footwear, 1955.

page 22: Hazards of stiletto heels, 1953.

page 25: Hungarian fashion shoes, 1973.

page 26: Shoeshine in Piccadilly Circus, London, 1981, Neil Libbert/The Observer/Hulton Getty Picture Collection.

page 28/29: Hobnailed boots, 1937.

page 30/31: Italian shoemaker Gino Becucci, 1971.

page 32: Modeling school, Manchester, England, 1954.

page 34/35: Giant shoe, filled with Christmas toys for children at the London Hospital, 1931.

page 36/37: Tim Curry as Frank N Furter in *The Rocky Horror Picture Show,* 1975.

page 38: American rock group The Tubes at London's Hammersmith Odeon, 1977.

page 39: Left to right, sandals at Ascot, 1947; outfit created by Tokyo designer Kansai Yamamoto, 1971.

page 41: Horse Guard in Whitehall, London, 1959.